The Book of When

Library of Congress Cataloging-in-Publication Data

Jaffé, Laura.
The book of when / by Laura Jaffé ; illustrated by François Cointe.
p. cm.
ISBN 978-0-8109-7240-7
1. Children's questions and answers.
2. Curiosities and wonders—Juvenile literature.
I. Cointe, François, ill. II. Title.

AG195.J24 2008
031.02—dc22
2007040259

Translated by Gita Daneshjoo
Originally published in French as *Le Livre des Comment*
in 2005 by Editions de la Martinière Jeunesse

Printed and bound in France
10 9 8 7 6 5 4 3 2 1

HNA
harry n. abrams, inc.
a subsidiary of La Martinière Groupe
115 West 18th Street
New York, NY 10011
www.hnabooks.com

The Book of When

Laura Jaffé

Illustrations by
François Cointe

Abrams Books for Young Readers
New York

Contents

When was chewing gum invented?

It turns out chewing gum wasn't invented by Mr. Bazooka or Mr. Bubble, but by our prehistoric ancestors. Paleolithic man chewed on resin, probably to clean his teeth and sweeten his breath.

Later, European explorers were surprised to see the inhabitants of Mexico happily chewing a strange gum from exotic trees.

Chewing gum as we know it only started being sold in the United States in the mid-nineteenth century, through the efforts of Thomas Adams. Adams brought gum from a sapodilla tree he found in Mexico to his local general store. Cut into thin strips and sold by the piece, this chewing gum was an immediate sensation among local children and their parents. Following this initial success, Thomas Adams came up with the brilliant idea of improving gum's taste by flavoring and sweetening it, and opened the first chewing gum factory.

YOU COULD HAVE WAITED UNTIL WE WERE EXTINCT TO INVENT THIS JUNK!

Chewing gum became popular all over the United States in the early twentieth century and made its triumphant entry into Europe with American soldiers during the Second World War.

It is currently the best-selling candy in the world, with an average consumption of nearly two packs a day per American!

When does an artist become **famous?**

Every artist dreams of being famous at some point! Yet we have no idea why some artists get famous while other, equally deserving ones remain unknown. Even as a child, Mozart was acclaimed a prodigy throughout Europe, but the painter van Gogh was only recognized several decades after his death.

For those who put their heart and soul into their art, the public eye is important. The ultimate goal in creating a painting, a poem, or a sculpture is to express one's deepest feelings and share them with one's contemporaries and also with future generations.

So why do some artists not become famous during their lifetime? Maybe because they aren't fortunate enough to cross paths with the people who could appreciate or help them? Or because their art is too far ahead of its time, too different from the art their contemporaries are used to seeing, reading, or hearing?

It's difficult to say why exactly, because there's no recipe for becoming famous and talent frequently isn't enough. The one thing that's certain is that an artist's life isn't as easy as it looks.

When will pigs fly?

Have you ever asked an adult when something will happen, and they've answered "when pigs fly"? It's a common expression meaning "not for a long, long time —if ever!"

Pigs are four-legged creatures that live very close to the ground. There's virtually no chance that a pig will ever grow wings and take off from the ground—unless you're living in a science fiction novel.

No one knows exactly where the expression comes from.

PIGS WILL FLY WHEN CHICKENS HAVE TEETH.

WATCH OUT FOR YOUR BACKSIDE!

But maybe it started because it's a particularly funny image. Imagine a pig—pink, round, with little short legs and a curlicue tail. Now imagine that pig with wings, oinking its way across the sky!

Other countries have similar expressions. In France, they say things will happen on "Saint Glinglin Day" (which doesn't exist), and in Hungary they say "when the cathedral is finished" (which, in the old days, could take hundreds of years).

When will I fall in love?

You can always pick the petals off a daisy to determine whether your friend, your parents, your great-uncle, or even your dog loves you or loves you not. But being in love is a whole other story!

Unlike the love we share with friends and family, falling in love overwhelms us with a passion so powerful it can make us both happy and unhappy.

You can be happy to have found your "soul mate," but sometimes you'll be unhappy because you can't have the one who's always in your thoughts by your side day and night. Because when you're madly in love, you want to share everything—to the point that you sometimes get the feeling you're losing your own identity.

A glance that turns you inside out, the connection you've always dreamed of, n irrepressible desire to constantly e with the person you love. There is no correct age to fall in love, though love at first sight at ten is a little different than it is at fifteen or thirty.

And though we often imagine that you need to be an adult to "really" be in love, once we're grown up we always look back to those first childhood love stories and remember the unmatchable intensity of the very first time.

DO YOU WANT TO BE MY BOYFRIEND?

WHAT'S THE HURRY?

9

When did painters start using paintbrushes?

Prehistoric painters were genuine artists who decorated cave walls with frescoes. They used paintbrushes, their fingers, stencils, or bellows to create their artwork.

Our prehistoric ancestors may not have developed the steam engine, but we can't deny that they were gifted inventors. Earlier than 10,000 BCE, they were already using sophisticated, ingenious tools such as the bone sewing needle and the deer hairbrush.

Their color palette consisted of what nature provided: red, ochre, and brown earth; certain relatively chalky rocks; and charcoal to outline their compositions in black.

Many cave paintings, such as those in the Lascaux Caves in France, have survived to the present day. Yet they sometimes remain enigmatic. While mammoths, horses, and bison are no mystery to us, we can only guess at the significance of the complex and strange geometric shapes that appear around them.

What if prehistoric painters had secrets to reveal to us?

YOU NEARLY DONE? HE'S GETTING TESTY.

GRRRR

When did people start looking at themselves in the mirror?

In fairy tales, mirrors often have strange powers. Alice went through the looking glass to continue her adventures in Wonderland, and every morning Snow White's cruel stepmother asked the mirror if she was still the most beautiful woman in the world. The magic of the mirror is it gives us the ability to look at ourselves "face to face," and see ourselves the way someone else would.

THEY SHOULD HAVE INVENTED THE MIRROR BEFORE THE RAZOR.

Before the invention of the mirror, men and women looked at their reflections on the smooth surface of a puddle or a pond, like beautiful Narcissus, who fell in love with his image and died of despair because he couldn't touch his other self.

The first mirrors were designed thousands of years ago. Until the fourteenth century, they were made of rounded polished metal. Then, as technical evolutions occurred, mirrors became increasingly flat. They were further improved by placing a piece of glass on a sheet of tin, and later, combinations of different metals were used.

Today the mirror is a familiar object that rules over our living rooms, bedrooms, bathrooms, and even our handbags. In amusement parks, fun house mirrors amuse and distort us.

Looking at yourself in the mirror is a way of confronting the truth: You can see how others see you; you can work on improving your image by putting on makeup, shaving, and getting dressed up; and you can measure the strength of your muscles!

When was the first sandwich made?

For an eighteenth-century English aristocrat, eating with one's fingers was unforgivably rude. Nonetheless, the very first sandwich was made in the castle of a lord in 1762.

On a dark winter evening, during his traditionally marathon card game with a group of friends, John Montagu, Earl of Sandwich, First Lord of His Majesty's Admiralty, wa once again faced with a terrible dilemma: Should he stop for dinner as his stomach demanded, or should he continue the game deep into the night?

A servant thought up the miraculous solution of bringing the master and his guests cold meat and cheese served between two slices of bread.

The players could keep playing cards without dirtying their hands! This simple, appealing recipe quickly spread throughout the county, then all over England.

Much later, at the 1904 World's Fair in Saint Louis, a modest Texan potter came up with the brilliant idea that would make his fortune and turn the United States into the international capital of sandwiches: For a few cents, he sold rolls containing ground beef seasoned with mustard, pickles, and onion. He called them hamburgers.

When did we learn to interpret dreams?

The Bible says that in a dream Pharaoh saw seven fat cows crossing a river followed by seven lean cows. His viceroy, Joseph, predicted that after seven years of prosperity seven years of famine would plague his kingdom.

In many cultures, dreams have been considered messages sent by the gods. In order to discover their meaning, people asked those who communicated with the heavens—such as prophets, druids, sorcerers or Native American shamans—to interpret them.

According to Freud, our dreams translate our deepest feelings—feelings so deep we may not even be aware of them—into pictures in a hidden part of our mind known as the unconscious.

In Western culture, we believe that dreams have a more personal significance. In 1900, the Austrian psychiatrist Sigmund Freud asserted that the strange stories that occupy our nights spring up from our most secret desires.

DID YOU DREAM THAT YOU WERE IN LOVE WITH A MERMAID AGAIN?

YES, BUT THIS TIME IT WAS MUCH BETTER. I HAD MY DIVING MASK AND MY FLIPPERS.

But beware! No dream dictionary holds the perfect key to your dreams for the simple reason that no one dreams the same way. If Peter dreams that he's swimming, it might mean that he feels comfortable in everyday life, happy as a clam, while the same dream might mean Paul feels like he's drowning.

When do we make a wish?

Long before us, the Persians touched wood when they expressed their wishes. They believed that the spirits of Fire and Vitality were capable of influencing people's fates living in the veins of tree trunks.

Opportunities to "make a wish" are found in every civilization, but each follows far different rituals.

The Japanese wish for their sick loved ones to get better by offering them one thousand folded paper cranes. Here in the United States, people throw coins into fountains to make wishes.

YOU'RE ENTITLED TO THREE WISHES.

THREE PER LAMP?

In every culture, making a wish means that we believe (or at least hope) that our act will have the magical power to turn our wishes into reality, just like in a fairy tale, where people make wishes come true simply by rubbing an enchanted lamp or reciting a miracle-working formula.

Fairy tales are meant to be imaginative—the writers don't have to worry about being realistic. On the other hand, believing that our real-life wishes are fated to come true as if by enchantment is a superstition that makes us run the risk of confusing our desires with reality.

When do volcanoes erupt?

Once upon a time, volcanic eruptions were both terrifying and unpredictable. Today, thanks to the hard work of vulcanologists, we can predict volcanic eruptions at least a few hours in advance and evacuate local populations early enough to avoid large casualties.

The center of the earth is very hot—so hot that rock melts into a liquid form. This bubbling, boiling liquid—called magma—releases a pressurized gas.

When this gas becomes too compressed, it escapes through cracks in the most fragile and thinnest parts of the earth's crust. This is where volcanoes form. Volcanoes project ash and lava (which is actually the magma) into the sky at temperatures reaching 1,800 degrees Fahrenheit. The ash and lava fall back on the ground in incandescent rivulets that engulf and burn everything in their path. This is what we call a volcanic eruption.

We've all heard of Pompeii, once a small vacation town for rich Romans that was completely buried in only a few minutes on a beautiful August morning in 79 CE.

That day, Mount Vesuvius erupted without any warning. The stunned inhabitants were trapped under several feet of lava and ash, frozen like stone statues for all eternity. Petrifying!

When was Coca-Cola invented?

Invented in 1886 by an American pharmacist in Atlanta, this famous drink incorporating coca leaves and cola nuts was initially sold as medicine. It was supposed to be a miracle cure for migraines, digestive problems, and all sorts of nervous disorders.

One day, the Atlanta pharmacist mistakenly substituted bubbly water for the usual flat water and added it to a dose of the medicinal syrup. This is how Coca-Cola as we know it came to be.

The first Coca-Cola advertisement boasted that the beverage was, "Coca-Cola. Delicious! Refreshing! Exhilarating! Invigorating!" Advertisement has always been the key to the soft drink's success. In the thirties, billboards featured a Coca-Cola–loving Santa Claus. During World War II, Coca-Cola ads launched a great patriotic campaign promising each U.S. soldier a free bottle of Coke no matter where he was in the world.

The other trick up Coca-Cola's sleeve is its secret recipe, a mixture of aromas mysteriously called 7X and kept in the vault of an Atlanta bank. No one has ever managed to replicate it.

Now you can find this "black gold" all over the world. Yet some people are turning away from the old medicine, accusing it of being too sweet—and bad for your health!

When will all the children in the world go to **school?**

In the United States, Europe, and many industrialized and wealthy countries around the world, school is compulsory and child labor has been illegal since the late nineteenth century.

But in other parts of the world, 200 to 300 million children are still working in frequently unsanitary, unsafe conditions.

In certain developing parts of the world where poverty pervades, school is a luxury limited to a few privileged children. Many kids in these areas never learn how to read or write. Starting at the age of five or six, they earn a pittance working ten to twelve hours a day in factories and sweatshops to help their families survive.

In China, children make fireworks; in Sierra Leone, they risk their lives mining for diamonds; in Benin, they work in cotton plantations; and in the Ivory Coast, they pick cocoa beans. In some countries like India and Haiti, children are even sold into slavery.

Children are forced to work due to extreme poverty. Let's hope we soon find a fairer way to share our planet's resources so that children all over the world can finally head to class.

When I feel down, why do I ransack the fridge?

An argument, a rainy Sunday afternoon that stretches on and on . . . It doesn't take much to get the blues. And when you're not feeling a hundred percent, you often console yourself with a few salty or sweet delights.

WHAT'S WRONG? WHAT DO YOU WANT? DO YOU NEED MY HELP?

I WANT MY FRIDGE!

The familiar taste of your favorite candy, a handful of chips, a chocolate bar, or a can of soda are the simple pleasures you can offer yourself by opening the treasure chest of the pantry or the fridge.

By filling your stomach, you momentarily chase away the feeling of emptiness and sadness that's come over you. And by consuming sugar—the slow sugar in starches or the fast sugar in candy—you give your brain the pick-me-up it craves when you're a little tired.

But beware! As Benjamin Franklin wrote in *Poor Richard's Almanack*, "Eat to live, and not live to eat!"

If you snack too much, your brain can no longer tell the difference between a genuine need to eat to "charge your batteries" and when you're being plain greedy. You wind up having the feeling that you're always a little hungry and lose the ability to regulate your appetite. It's best to beware of the extra calories.

When are we sure we're right?

Even though our senses can mislead us by making us believe a mirage is a beautiful green oasis, some basic truths—such as two plus two equals four and strawberries are red—are undeniable. If we started doubting everything, we'd go crazy.

Yet we don't have answers for every question. Sometimes it's wisest to agree with the Greek philosopher Socrates that, "The only thing I know is that I know nothing." And that it's useless to always want to be right!

After all, what does being right really mean? Sometimes what's true for you isn't necessarily true for others. This is certainly the case when you say something is "beautiful" or "good," making affirmations entirely based on your taste and standards.

Even when you're absolutely sure you're right, it may be wise to listen to those who disagree. According to a saying perfect for stubborn people all over the world, "Only fools never change their minds."

As for the great philosophical questions the human race has always wrestled with—*Does God exist? Is there life after death? What's the meaning of life?*—they exceed our ability to be certain. In such cases, it's best to replace "I know" with "I believe."

When did history begin?

NO WRITING, NO HISTORY.

SCHOOL WAS GREAT IN THE NEOLITHIC AGE!

Historians trace the beginning of history, which comes after prehistory, to the appearance of writing.

Thanks to the development of writing, each generation could now leave the next generations an account of what it had lived through: discoveries, explorations, wars, and conquests. The first form of writing was invented in Mesopotamia around 3500 BCE. A more elaborate form, the hieroglyph, was developed in Egypt, while the calligram was first used in China. Step by step, writing based on alphabets evolved all around the world.

Man initially recorded his history on stone, papyrus, and parchment. It wasn't until thousands of years later, in fifth-century BCE Greece, that history became a genuinely precise and rigorous science.

Herodotus, the "Father of History," said that it was important to distinguish between what was real and what was imaginary in tales of the past. He titled his nine books *The Histories* and dedicated himself to accurately relating events without including any mytholo or poetry, "so that time does not abolish the work of men.

Since then, historians have tirelessly aimed for the same goal: to constitute the most accurate memory of the human adventure possible, to keep track of it, and learn the lessons from the past that will ensure we make tomorrow better than yesterday.

When did people start taking vacations?

Three cheers for vacations, workers' well-deserved chance to get some rest! But did you know that not so long ago people didn't take vacations because employers didn't pay for them?

How could people give up a week's salary to go to the beach? Whether you were an office worker, a car repairman, or a salesman, your only days off the whole year long were Sundays and legal holidays. Only the rich could enjoy the luxury of taking a break without calculating what it cost them.

In many countries, the government requires employers to provide a certain number of weeks of paid vacation. In the United States, there is no law about vacations, but many employers offer two weeks or more per year. When this change went into effect, it was an authentically revolutionary change in people's way of life—they were actually going to be paid to do nothing!

DOWN WITH PAID VACATIONS!

EVERY YEAR THEY ABANDON US.

Little by little, families that had never traveled beyond their neighborhood, their city, or their region were able to pile into packed trains to set astonished eyes on the seaside, the countryside, or the mountains.

Children— who had three months of school vacation—discovered the joys of summer camp, where you can have a good time far away from your parents.

When does my face turn red?

Whether we turn tomato red or even beet red, our faces get red because our emotions are working full blast. If we're flushed with anger, embarrassment, or shyness, the color creeping over our faces reveals a violent emotion we'd much rather keep to ourselves.

This excessive redness, which is due to a sudden dilation of the small blood vessels in our face, can be a real annoyance.

Unfortunately, we have no way of controlling this untimely phenomenon. It is related to the part of our nervous system that controls involuntary actions such as breathing, digesting, and what we refer to as the sympathetic system.

Sometimes, a sympathetic system can get carried away. It accelerates our heartbeat, makes us sweat excessively, and turns our whole face as red as a fire truck.

When fear of blushing develops into a real phobia, it becomes a psychological illness known as erythrophobia. It pushes those who suffer from it to avoid any situation where they might get flushed in public. They're too scared to go to class or work or to meet with a group of friends. They require treatment to slowly resume a normal life in society.

WHY IS YOUR FACE ALL GREEN?

DID SOMETHING SCARE YOU?

DID YOU EAT A POISONOUS MUSHROOM?

BLUSHING IS TOUGH, BUT IT MAKES YOU SEE RED WHEN YOUR FRIENDS ARE COLOR-BLIND.

When the sun disappears, where does it hide?

For a long time, people only believed in what they could see. And since every night they saw the sun disappear beyond the horizon, they were convinced that great fireball was going to bed to rest until the next morning . . . just like you and me!

If the sun was masked by a lunar eclipse and disappeared for a few minutes in the middle of the day, people cried out that divine retribution was upon them and the end of the world was near. In Asia, people believed an evil dragon was trying to eat the sun every time there was an eclipse. Men shot arrows into the sky until the defeated celestial monster finally released the sun.

Until the end of the Middle Ages, people believed that the earth was the center of the universe and that day and night alternated as the sun revolved around the earth.

It wasn't until the sixteenth century that Copernicus, a Polish astronomer, put forward his revolutionary hypothesis: It isn't the sun that revolves around the earth, but the earth that revolves around the sun. Day and night are due to the earth's rotations, rather than the sun's movements around the earth.

No matter how many "jaw-dropping" sunsets we see, the truth is that the sun never goes to bed. We earth-dwellers are the ones who turn our backs on it every night.

IT'S LATE, I'M GOING TO BED.

YOU'RE LUCKY... I STILL HAVE TO GO LIGHT UP CHINA.

When should we disobey rules?

Children have to obey adults, and everyone has to obey the law. Don't steal, don't be violent, respect public property, don't insult or mistreat others.

In most cases, we gladly accept these obligations and prohibitions— they make life in society possible. Without rules, society would be subjected to the laws of the jungle and the dictatorship of the strongest.

Yet there are certain circumstances in which it is wise to disobey. We should always pay attention when our conscience suggests an order is unjust, and we should refuse to obey it. What is legal, or authorized by law, is not necessarily what is legitimate, or just.

History is full of examples of disobedience that were actually acts of resistance to barbaric tyranny. During the civil rights movement in the sixties, many activists chose civil disobedience rather than obeying prejudiced laws and practices. Martin Luther King Jr. was a big proponent of civil disobedience.

Similarly, Nelson Mandela spent decades illegally fighting the racist laws of South Africa so that blacks could enjoy the same rights as whites. When faced with an inhumane law or an unjust or unjustified order, disobedience is not only a right, it is an obligation.

When did we realize that children are people?

Once upon a time, people thought children should be whipped into shape like little animals rather than be educated. In the eighteenth century, philosophers such as Jean-Jacques Rousseau became interested in children's personalities and in what they were able to learn and understand at various stages of their growth.

Little by little, children came to be considered people who also have rights along with their obligations.

LIE DOWN!

SLEEP!

NOW!

DAD, WE'RE NOT ANIMALS.

WE'RE PEOPLE.

In 1989, a little over two hundred years after the Declaration of Independence, these rights were put down in writing in the Convention on the Rights of the Child, a legal document adopted by many countries. The Convention states that children must be educated, protected, housed, properly fed, shielded from bad treatment, and given the opportunity to play.

Today, children in democratic countries have a certain number of obligations that actually correspond to specific rights. For instance, the obligation to go to school is based on the right to an education.

If you're ever reluctant to go to class, never forget that children all over the planet dream about learning to read, write, and count instead of going to work to help their families survive.

When did people start wearing eyeglasses?

Introduced in the thirteenth century, eyeglasses are now indispensable accessories to about one out of every two people on the planet. But how did people who didn't have good eyesight read before the invention of glasses?

I INVENTED THE CONTACT LENS!

Rich Romans had educated slaves read to them, while medieval monks used "reading stones"—enormous magnifying glasses they moved over the parchment they were reading.

A Franciscan monk named Roger Bacon devised the first eyeglasses, which consisted of lenses with wood frames held together by a single nail. These early glasses could only help people who had difficulty seeing close objects. It wasn't until the sixteenth century that opticians were able to correct myopia, which was then only known as "shortsightedness."

In fact, the advent of contact lenses and, more recently, laser operations to improve eyesight leads one to wonder if eyeglasses won't soon be relegated to the antiquarian wing of museums. But we'll always have sunglasses, the essential accessories of movie stars.

Since then, optical techniques have improved with the invention of temple arms in the eighteenth century, and of lenses made of light, durable plastic in the twentieth century.

29

When was **Europe founded?**

From a geographical point of view, Europe has existed since before human beings walked the earth, back when th continents formed. But the idea of a Europe o the people—a large fed eration of united, allie countries—is very recent.

Though the idea first appeared in the eighteenth century, it wasn't until after World War II, when most European countries were devastated by war, that people were ready to accept British prime minister Winston Churchill's advice that "We must build a kind of United States of Europe."

From the very beginning, the unified Europe has been a Europe of peace. This new Europe, which is no longer strictly geographic but political, has opened itself to new members and has thus fa been able to avoid armed conflict within its borders.

The Europe Churchill dreamed of has slowly become a reality and has greatly evolved in the last few years. With twenty-seven member countries, the European Union has become a political and economic power that can rival the United States. Though they speak twenty different languages, Europeans feel a little more European every day.

Today, every young European's future is wide open. One could graduate from high school in Madrid; study in Hamburg; work in London, Athens, or Brussels; and retire in Lisbon.

When do we yawn?

We yawn when we're hungry, tired, or bored. Yawning is an essential natural reflex that babies acquire in the fifth month of pregnancy.

When we yawn, we relax tired muscles in our jaw and our rib cage and all the way out to our arms and legs.

Yawning causes a pleasant sensation and wakes us up for a few seconds. Even animals yawn to fight sleepiness and remain alert when they need to hunt or defend themselves.

As with all bodily functions we can't control—such as burping and passing gas—yawning is considered impolite in Western societies. As children, we learn to put our hands over our mouths when we yawn. But in the past, people put their hands over their mouths to ensure that their souls didn't escape from their bodies, and to avoid giving evil spirits a chance to get through this wide open door and infect them with a string of illnesses. Funny, isn't it?

WHY DO I HAVE TO PUT MY HAND IN FRONT OF MY MOUTH WHEN I YAWN?

GUESS!

No one knows exactly what happens to our bodies when we yawn. We do know, though, that yawns are highly contagious. When you see someone else yawn, you'll almost always end up yawning yourself!

When will we have a month of Sundays?

In ancient Greece, one week lasted ten days and there was no specific day assigned for resting.

The Jewish week, which was later adopted by Christians and Muslims, lasts seven days: the amount of time God took to create the world (six days) and rest (the seventh day).

What about a month of Sundays?

It has never figured in any calendar and has never existed outside the expression, which means "a very long time." Sunday got its name back in Roman times, when days were named after the planets—Monday (Moon), Saturday (Saturn), and Sunday (Sun), for example.

In Christian tradition, Sunday is the day of rest. A month of Sundays sounds pretty relaxing—but it's unlikely to happen for a long, long time.

I'LL TAKE FOUR SATURDAYS AND THREE SUNDAYS...

OR THE OPPOSITE.

When did we start burying the dead?

Unlike animals, human beings have always made a point of paying tribute to the dead through a wide variety of pagan and religious funeral rites.

Archeologists have discovered prehistoric tombs more than eighty thousand years old. In these tombs, the deceased was buried under a flat stone surrounded by his weapons, tools, and food as if he needed to approach death with everything required to survive!

Later, the Egyptians came to believe that to ensure the deceased eternal life in the hereafter it was necessary to prevent the body from decomposing by mummifying it.

They removed the internal organs and preserved the dead body in salt, then covered it in ointments before wrapping it in hundreds of feet of thin strips of fabric.

Following the advent of the great monotheistic religions (religions dedicated to a single God), Jewish, Muslim, and Christian funerary customs were less concerned with what became of the body—the only important thing is the soul and what happens to it after death. The body is simply buried without any attempt at conserving it and cemeteries serve as places for the deceased's loved ones to reflect and remember.

When will I stop being jealous?

Jealousy isn't always easy to handle. We're a little ashamed to recognize that deep down we're envious of the growing friendship between our two best friends, or that we resent our little sister for being our grandparents' favorite.

Jealousy is completely natural, but it puts us in a position of weakness. Saying "I'm jealous" is admitting that we're incapable of enjoying the happiness and success of those we love and that we envy them instead. Once we become conscious of our jealousy, we yearn to get rid of that nasty feeling.

Where do these overwhelming, embarrassing feelings of jealousy come from? They're often due to a lack of confidence in our ability to be loved and to find our place among our peers.

Instead of letting yourself be eaten alive by this destructive plague—of dreaming of throwing your little sister in the Dumpster, your big brother into a poison ivy patch, and your classmate rivals onto Mars—maybe it would be better to accept yourself as you are and put your best qualities forward. Then you'd see that you don't have so much to be envious of, and that you don't lose anything by sharing.

When was school made compulsory?

School has existed since ancient history, but for thousands of years there were no laws to oblige parents to send their sons and daughters to school.

School was a luxury reserved for a handful of boys from the richest echelons of society. Girls and poor children of both sexes were excluded and remained at home to help around the house or work in the fields. And that's the way it was for a long time!

The first state in the United States to regulate compulsory schooling was Massachusetts in 1852. Each state has its own policy regarding school, but most require that you attend school until the age of sixteen.

TO SCHOOL

THEY CAN'T EXPECT US TO NEED ALL THESE BOOKS...

I'M GOING TO STAY HOME!

Some students choose to go to a private school rather than public, and some are home-schooled by their parents or a tutor, but everyone must get some kind of education.

Saying that school is compulsory also serves as a reminder that every student should be in class, not playing hooky, and that overly frequent, unexplained absences can lead to severe sanctions.

When are stars blue?

Stars seem tiny to us because of the vast distance that separates us from them. But in fact they are enormous balls of incredibly hot gas that are perpetually exploding.

Stars spit light and heat like massive cosmic fireworks until, having burned off all their hydrogen reserves, they extinguish and die.

Yet if you really look closely, you'll see that this is not totally true. Stars shine across a subtle spectrum ranging from white to red through blue and orange. If we carefully observe the sky on a clear night, the roughly six thousand stars visible from Earth shine in every color.

BLUE.

WHITE.

YELLOW.

RED.

ALL THIS TO WIND UP AS A BLACK HOLE!

Even with your eyes closed you'd swear that stars are pale yellow, just as sure as strawberries are red and zebras are black and white.

Earth's own star, the sun, which is of medium size and temperature, is yellow. Betelgeuse is red and Sirius and Vega are blue. In fact, the color of a star is related to its temperature. Strangely enough, the hottest stars shine in cold colors such as white and blue, while the coldest stars are in warmer tints such as orange and red.

When did people start paying for things with money?

Imagine a world without money: To get a new pair of shoes, you'd have to trade three DVDs, several pounds of candy, and a schoolbag. This type of trading, known as bartering, was used long ago, before the invention of coins. People met their needs by exchanging objects they made, vegetables they grew, cattle they raised, and even marriageable young women in their families.

SALARY: HE SAID WE'D GET THIRTY LASHES . .

I'D RATHER BE PAID IN DOLLARS.

Later, as trade developed, people decided to make things easier by using precious goods that were easy to store, divide, and weigh as currency. Salt was the first currency and was later replaced by metals such as gold, silver, brass, and bronze.

In 500 BCE, Croesus, a king in Asia Minor, came up with the brilliant idea to have a few gold and silver coins struck with a sign indicating their value. From then on, it was no longer necessary to weigh the metal to determine its value. Only the king decided the value of money.

With the invention of bills in the Middle Ages and of checks and credit cards in the twentieth century, money continued to circulate more easily, without weighing down our wallets.

Does your grandfather ever ask if you want some silver to buy candy? Our coins haven't been made with silver since 1965!

When
do we need to wash
our hands?

In every religious tradition, whether Jewish or Muslim, Christian or Hindu, washing your hands is a rite used to purify the body so you're free of the dirt of everyday life when addressing your prayers to God.

For many centuries, people did not realize how important it was for their health to wash their hands with soap. Before the nineteenth century, they didn't know that illnesses were due to small microscopic organisms, germs, and that you need to wash regularly to get rid of them.

Many women died in childbirth due to devastating infections they caught from midwives who didn't wash their hands before helping them deliver. Doctors passed from one operating table to the next without stopping by the sink, sometimes even going straight from a corpse to another patient, thereby dooming him to the same fate.

Nowadays, everyone knows that washing your hands is essential to maintaining good hygiene. Surgeons wash their hands for ten minutes with a brush and special soap before they enter the operating room.

I FORESEE A SERIOUS DISEASE IF YOU KEEP SUCKING YOUR THUMB.

In regular life, we wash our hands several times a day—before we cook or sit down to eat, after we've been to the bathroom, after we've gotten dirty, before we take a newborn in our arms, or before looking through this book, especially if we've just eaten a chocolate bar!

When were ballpoint pens invented?

Before the twentieth century, people relied on quills and fountain pens to write their thoughts. Quills were first made of feathers because the ink could gather in the hollow center. They were popularized in the eighth century CE.

After quills came fountain pens, which were shaped like quills but were made of metal and came with their own reservoir of ink. Instead of dipping the sharpened end of a feather into a pot of ink, people could hold the pen in their hand—making the device much more portable.

However, fountain pens still had problems. They were prone to leaks, spots, and smudging. The methods of refilling the reservoir were often cumbersome and messy. The world needed a new type of writing instrument.

In 1938, László Bíró, a Hungarian newspaper editor, filed a patent for a new kind of pen. This one had a reservoir like the fountain pen, but a suspended rolling ball at the end of the pen kept the ink flowing at a steady rate.

This ballpoint pen exploded in popularity. It was easy to use and cheap to produce. In many areas of the world, ballpoints are still called after their creator—Biros.

When does life start?

In Chinese culture, a child's age is calculated not from the date of its birth but from the presumed date of its conception.

A few hours after the coupling of a man and a woman, the future father's spermatozoa fertilizes the future mother's ovum to form an egg even smaller than the period at the end of this sentence.

5, 4, 3, 2, 1...

GO!

After seven days, this tiny egg will nestle in the mother's uterus, where it will grow and develop for the next nine months. During its time as a fetus, it learns to recognize its parents' voices, suck its thumb, and wiggle around. When the baby is born, it experiences the world for the first time.

The question of when life begins is very controversial, and many people have strong views on the subject. It is something you will have to think about very hard—there's no answer accepted by everyone.

So when does life begin? At fertilization? A few hours, days, or three months later? And is the beginning of a life as a tiny embryo really also the beginning of the person? These questions will always be very difficult to answer.

When was Santa Claus born?

We know the birth dates of Louis XIV, George Washington, Mark Twain, and Leonardo da Vinci's, but we don't know when Santa Claus was born! Unlike contemporary celebrities, that legendarily generous, debonair old man has always remained very discreet about his private life.

In the days of your great-grandparents, Santa Claus's ancestor Saint Nicholas brought gifts to well-behaved European children on December 6. In France, he traveled with the mean Père Fouettard, who took care of punishing kids who had been really bad. Some European countries still celebrate Saint Nicholas Day.

In 1931, Santa Claus entered the advertising business and became a star. He was seen strutting around on Coca-Cola billboards, wearing the soft drink's trademark red and white the first time while taking a few sips the celebrated beverage to regain his strength and get back to distributing toys. About fifteen years later, Santa Claus made his triumphant entry into Europe.

Santa Claus first appeared in the nineteenth century as a character created by American author Clement Clarke Moore and *Harper's Weekly* illustrator Thomas Nast. He was soon well-known to thousands of American kids.

WHERE WERE YOU BORN? IN A CABBAGE PATCH?

YES, BUT A RED CABBAGE PATCH.

And ever since that time, in many countries, the modern pagan character of Santa Claus has been stealing the spotlight from the infant Jesus on his very own birthday, December 25!

When are we allowed to lie?

At first glance, we'd be tempted to answer, "Never!"

The edifying tale of the Italian puppet Pinocchio, whose nose got a little longer every time he told a lie, reminds us that it's not right to lie. The law severely penalizes some lies, such as bearing false witness or making untrue statements under oath.

Nonetheless, some things are better left unsaid. Every language in the world has a whole range of sayings to remind us that in some cases, "saying the truth is losing the friendship" (Russia), and that it is often "better to lie than to speak ill" (India).

SO PINOCCHIO, DO YOU THINK I'M BEAUTIFUL? AND PLEASE DON'T LIE!

UM...

Should you tell your grandmother that you really love her but sometimes you find her company excruciatingly boring? Should you inform your best friend, in the name of honesty, that you hate her new haircut? Or your neighbor in English class that he smells bad? Sometimes it's better to lie by omission—painful truths are always better left unsaid, if only out of politeness.

But before you swear on your mother that you saw honest-to-goodness aliens getting a tan on the beach or you assure the teacher that the dog ate your math homework for breakfast, remember that there are some circumstances where the simplest thing to do is to tell the truth.

When
do we get a
tooth pulled?

In the Middle Ages, if a cavity became too painful to bear, people went to find the "tooth puller" who worked on the market square.

Standing among the vegetable stalls and the poultry, the tooth puller used a pair of pliers to tear out the diseased tooth without washing his hands or using any anesthetic. People grouped together to watch the tooth puller at work and left a few coins behind. He was a popular character who told tall tales to amuse passersby and was accompanied by musicians playing the cymbal and drums to cover the cries of the unhappy patient.

WHICH TOOTH DO YOU WANT ME TO PULL?

THESE!

Thankfully, dentistry, like medicine, has made amazing progress over the last few centuries, gradually evolving from a charlatan's trade to a highly specialized profession. Thanks to the invention of X-ray photography, anesthetics, and tools such as the dreaded dentist's drill, we can care for sick teeth rather than systematically pulling them out.

Extraction is now a last resort for teeth that are simply too far gone to save, or for wisdom teeth when the jaw is too small to make room for them.

And every dentist agrees—the key to having healthy teeth is to brush them morning and night, after breakfast and after dinner.

45

When did theater start?

In the beginning, theater was an outdoor free party that was open to everyone.

In ancient Greece, masked and made-up men acted out episodes from the lives of gods and mythological heroes before a massive open-air audience that gathered for ten days a year. At the end, the raucous audience selected the best show.

In the Middle Ages, the church organized per-formance festivals to spread knowledge of religious history. At that time, adults and children alike could be found rejoicing at the sight of an actor disguised as Saint Francis standing in front of a cathedral next to a bear trainer or a barker.

From the Renaissance to the nineteenth century, the theater left the street and shut itself into small dark rooms you had to pay to get into. It became a form of entertainment for the rich, reserved for cultured indi-viduals. For the first time, actresses joined actors onstage. Some audience members were scandalized while others applauded the change.

What about now? Every year when the nice weather rolls around, wonderful festivals show us that outdoor performances are back in fashion.

When is there war?

In the United States, people less than sixty years old have never experienced a world war. The sad memories of destruction, fear, and deprivation elderly people tell us about seem to belong to a distant era.

TODAY WE'RE GOING TO HAVE A WAR.

WHY?

BECAUSE TODAY I'M THE STRONGEST.

Yet despite the efforts of international organizations (such as the UN) to maintain peace, wars continue to break out all over the world. If everyone aspires to live in peace, why do we still make war?

Some countries declare war to enlarge their territory, to appropriate the resources they covet, or to impose their ways of living and worshipping.

Others go to war because they believe that the land they live on belongs only to them and they don't want to share it. Sometimes there can even be a civil war within a single country, between different ethnic groups or partisans of conflicting political beliefs.

Many countries argue for durable peace and sign alliances and nonaggression pacts, yet continue to build increasingly sophisticated and destructive weapons. They hope that if they're armed to the teeth no one will dare to attack them. But is armed peace really danger-free?

When
can you see a
shooting star?

Listen up stargazers and superstitious people: Word has it that if you see a shooting star your most secret wishes come true.

So long as it's a clear, moonless night and you're far from city lights, you can see an average of seven shooting stars an hour.

But did you know that shooting stars aren't really stars? They're debris from celestial rocks crossing the atmosphere and crashing to earth at a breakneck speed of several dozens of miles per second.

By rubbing up against air molecules at high speeds, these small extraterrestrial rocks become extremely hot and burst into flames. Once they're burning, they look like tiny stars leaving trails of fire in their wake.

Shooting stars are generally very small: They're about the size of a pea, or even of a grain of sand, and only shine for a few seconds before being extinguished. But some can weigh more than two pounds at the moment they enter the earth's atmosphere. These shooting stars produce a considerably brighter, more sustained light than their celestial "little sisters."

SPLASH

OH! A SHOOTING STAR!

VERY FUNNY.

When are you too fat, too tall, or too short?

"Fatty!" "Beanpole!" "Midget!" If you happen not to be of standard height or weight, you may be regularly subjected to foolish, cruel teasing.

When you look at yourself in the mirror, you may get down on yourself for being too fat, too tall, or too short . . . in other words, for not having a model's body.

But what kind of world would we live in if everyone looked as though they were made from the same mold? The hereditary traits we've received from our parents make us all different. All these little physical and moral differences are what make each of us unique and irreplaceable.

Where do these beauty standards that vary from one time period to another, and from one country to another, come from anyhow? For a long time, a woman had to be chubby to be considered beautifu in Europe. Today, being thin is the be-all an end-all in Western societies, while in Afric and India, curves are seen as a sign of good health and remain highly appreciated. In Cameroon, there's even a beauty contest for women who weigh a minimum of 175 pounds!

HOW CAN YOU BE A MODEL? YOU'RE TOO THIN!

What is or isn't beautiful is like what's in fashion—it comes and goes. You're better off counting on your friends—your real friends— whose warm way of looking at you helps you to love yourself the way you are.

When do languages die?

Whether it's English, Chinese, Wolof, Hindi, Arabic, French, or Swahili, a language only stays alive because we speak it. When a language is no longer spoken, it begins to die out, generation by generation, until it is completely forgotten.

IS IT SERIOUS, DOCTOR?

CONSIDERING YOU'RE FRENCH, YES.

A language generally dies when the civilization that gave birth to it disappears. For instance, Latin gradually stopped being spoken after the fall of the Roman Empire.

Other regional languages slowly lose their importance in favor of the national culture. Some countries mandate a national language that everyone must learn.

Some language specialists—who are known as linguists—are worried that the diversity of languages is threatened. Some predict that by 2100, half the languages currently spoken in the world will have been replaced by English, Spanish, Chinese, and Arabic.

English is one of the most popular languages in the world. In many countries, people speak their native language and English. Chinese is becoming more universal as well—after all, 1.3 billion people speak it or one of its dialects.

When will space stop growing?

Imagine that the universe and all its galaxies, separated by several thousands of light-years, are a gigantic balloon gradually getting bigger and bigger: The universe grows constantly and its galaxies gradually grow farther apart.

According to scientists, the universe was created some 15 billion years ago. It appeared suddenly as a ball of gas and tiny burning dust particles. Then there was the gigantic explosion known as the "Big Bang."

Since then, the universe has gotten progressively colder and galaxies and stars have formed within it, but it hasn't stopped growing. Won't it stop growing one of these days? This is a question many astrophysicists are investigating. Currently, their answers are only hypotheses.

The first hypothesis is a disaster scenario known as the "Big Crunch": The universe becomes too heavy and eventually collapses on itself and self-destructs. Second possibility: Having become increasingly light by diluting itself in space, the universe will grow more quickly.

We'd like to bank on the least dramatic theory: The universe will calmly keep doing what it's doing at a relatively steady pace through the immensity of space-time.

When do we have hiccups?

You'll come up with anything to try to get rid of the hiccups—getting your best friend to scare you, drinking a glass of water upside down, eating a sugar cube dipped in vinegar.

But even though they're annoying, hiccups aren't serious unless they last for a whole day or recu[r] too frequently.

But why and how do we get the hiccups? Often, we get them when we've eaten too much or too quickly, without taking the time to chew properly.

HEAR THAT? THE BABY HAS THE HICCUPS!

IT NEEDS TO DRINK THIS GLASS OF VINEGAR WITH ITS HEAD UPSIDE DOWN.

HIPS!
HIPS!
HIPS!

Swallowing too much at once, or eating food that's too hot, irritates the nerves that control the muscles in your respiratory channels. The muscles contract involuntarily and the glottis closes abruptly. When you inhale, this muscle movement provokes the characteristic, funny sound that startles us and regularly interrupts our speech.

Babies frequently get the hiccups after sucking down a bottle's worth of milk too quickly. Sometimes you can even feel a fetus gently hiccupping inside its mother's belly, which is where we get the saying, "A child who hiccups is a healthy child."

When
do we need an
ID card?

In many countries around the world, it's illegal to walk around without carrying documents that prove your identity and nationality.

Yet for many centuries, people lived and died without having their first and family names or date and place of birth officially recorded.

Catholics only had their baptism certificates, while in Africa people counted on the memory of a griot, a kind of village historian who orally transmitted the history of the village and its inhabitants from one generation to the next.

In the past, it used to be far more important to belong to a village, a profession, a religious order, a family line, or a clan than to a country. And since everyone knew one another in these small groups, there was no need to show identification to prove who you were.

In the United States, people can get an ID card or a driver's license if they properly prove their identity. In order to travel to other countries, citizens must apply for a passport, which proves that you are a citizen and free to travel.

When did the first **humans** appear?

Humans have always tried to answer the "big questions": Where do we come from and who created us? What is our origin?

IN 200 MILLION YEARS, YOU'LL BE A MAN, MY SON.

YES, FATHER.

In the nineteenth century, science succeeded in shedding light on a significant aspect of the mystery of our origins. The British biologist Charles Darwin developed a revolutionary theory: Humans were not created as they are by God, but are a link in the evolution of animal species. According to Darwin, we humans are related to the chimpanzee.

As far back as recorded memory, every civilization has tried to answer these questions with stories such as the myth of Adam and Eve—shared by the Jewish, Christian, and Muslim faiths.

About five million years ago, the large African monkeys stood up, began walking on two legs, and gradually lost their fur.

About three million years later, the first humans appeared. Modern scientists named this new species of mammal, our direct ancestor, the *Homo erectus*. These humans constructed stone tools and knew how to use fire. Finally, two hundred thousand years ago, *Homo sapiens*, the "wise man," appeared. *Homo sapiens* could think, imagine, organize themselves into a society, believe, and create—in other words, they were men and women just like you or me, with some extra hairs.

When do frogs croak?

Ribbit, ribbit. When a frog croaks in a fairy tale, you know it's a prince transformed by an evil witch.

He is left to wait for the tender kiss of a princess to turn him back into a human.

In real life, frogs croaking and jumping up and down in the humid grass at the edge of a pond are also asking for love. They are calling female frogs to attract them to the water where they can lay their eggs.

So Mrs. Frog doesn't croak; only Mr. Frog emits a croaking singsong. To do so, he must contract his vocal cords while breathing and simultaneously expanding the vocal sac under his mouth, which serves as a resonance chamber like the one on a bagpipe.

Did you know that in the Middle Ages there was a strange profession known as "frog silencing"? The frog silencer's job was to keep frogs quiet by hitting the surface of the water so their croaking didn't bother the great and powerful people sleeping in nearby castles.

When will the sun stop shining?

Like every other star, the sun is not immortal. Born about 4.6 billion years ago, it is about halfway through its life—it will keep shining for roughly 5 billion more years.

But why do stars like our sun have to die one day?

GOOD NIGHT!

The sun, which is about 108 times bigger than the earth, is an enormous ball of extremely hot gas. As it burns, it is gradually exhausting its reserves of a gas called hydrogen. When this hydrogen is used up, the sun will expand to fifty times its current size and will become a very big star known as a red giant.

The sun will swallow up and burn Mercury and Venus and come closer to our planet. Earth will become so hot that life here will be impossible. Then the sun will get smaller and become a white dwarf that will slowly cool down over a period of several billion years until it is completely extinguished.

In a very, very distant future, the sun will stop shining. But elsewhere in the universe, in other galaxies, other stars may spend a few billion years warming up planets similar to our earth that are possibly, just possibly, just as nice to live on.

When will I have kids?

Children all over the world play Mommy and Daddy to imagine a distant future when they too will be parents. Having kids means being a grown-up and joining the chain of generations that makes each of us a link in the long history of humanity.

WHEN I GROW UP I WANT TO HAVE FIVE KIDS.

AND A BIG CAR TO PUT THEM IN.

Biologically, we are able to have sexual intercourse and conceive a child beginning in puberty. But most people who have just started puberty aren't ready for the responsibility of taking care of a child.

In some African and Asian countries, where contraceptive methods that allow people to have sex without running the risk of reproducing are seldom used, and people traditionally get married young, it isn't unusual to become a parent at fifteen or sixteen.

In industrialized countries like the United States, widely used birth control methods have given couples the option to choose the best time to have children—when they're twenty, thirty, forty, or even never. To each his own.

In fact, not everyone is ready to have kids at the same age: No matter how old you are, being ready to be a mother or a father means committing to taking care of your child and protecting and loving it.

59

When will we be able to take a walk on Mars?

What will happen in 2030, when, according to scientists' predictions, humans will first set foot on Mars? What will they discover at the end of their 186 million-mile journey?

Turn on the news in twenty-two years and find out! For the time being, only two robots, Spirit and Opportunity, have walked on Mars. They were sent by NASA in 2003 and regularly sent back strange and beautiful extra-terrestrial postcards.

The Martian landscape includes red deserts swept by gusts of wind, gigantic volcanoes, abrupt gorges, and breathtaking sunsets. But is there life on Mars?

For the moment, the red planet whose temperatures drop to -148 degrees Fahrenheit at night shows no sign of little green men or, more seriously, bacteria such as those that were necessary for the beginning of life on Earth.

Nonetheless, the discovery of ancient traces of liquid water (an element favorable to the blossoming of life) detected underground on Mars leaves us to suppose that life could have existed elsewhere than in the wild fantasies of comic book writers, movie directors, and novelists.

Let's keep hoping that one of these days we find our Martian cousins up there in the cold.

When did **women** win the right to **vote?**

It wasn't too long ago that women did not have the same rights as men in many civilized countries—and there are many places in the world where women are still treated as second-class citizens. Women began asserting their right to "suffrage"—that is, the right to vote—in the United States in the 1820s.

However, women's suffrage in the United States was not made into law until 1920. It was passed as the Nineteenth Amendment to the Constitution. Some states had allowed women to vote before then, but ever since, that right has been guaranteed for all citizens.

In the United Kingdom, women were specifically disenfranchised (not allowed to vote) in 1832. Not until 1928 did women get the same voting rights as men in the United Kingdom.

Why weren't women allowed to vote, and why are women still treated so poorly in many areas of the world? It was commonly believed (and still is, in many places) that women are inferior to men and do not have the judgment to make their own decisions.

Of course, you know that women can make decisions just as well as men. There's proof all around us!

YOU FORGOT TO GO IN THE BOOTH.

OOPS! SORRY.

When will I die?

When will I die, and what will I die of? We've all asked ourselves these questions at some point or another.

A lot of us are scared of death, the mysterious "last journey" from which no one has ever returned to tell us what it was like.

ARE YOU SCARED OF DEATH?

NOPE...

We have a hard time imagining that the world could keep going without us. We're scared of suffering, of being nothing, and of being eternally separated from those we love. Sometimes we even dream of discovering the fountain of youth. But there's no way to escape death, for it is part of life.

Should we really be afraid of death? For believers of most religions, death is not a cause for despair because it is not the ultimate end. Whether the soul rises up to the sky or is reincarnated in a new body or the deceased continues to live among us as a spirit, life after death can even promise great joy.

And if you don't believe in any God or a form of afterlife, you can convince yourself, as the philosopher Epicurus did, that "Death is nothing to us, since when we are, death has not come, and when death has come, we are not." In this case, life is lived in the present and is an opportunity that must be enjoyed at every moment.

When will **birds stop** being a sign **of spring?**

In the earth's temperate regions, people have always known that spring was on the way when they saw swallows or other birds fly overhead.

SPRING? HERE?

WE DON'T BRING WINTER TO YOUR PLACE!

The return of migratory birds that had left to spend the winter in a warmer climate always announced the return of pleasant weather.

But now that global warming is speeding up due to air pollution caused by greenhouse gas emissions from heavy industry and automobile exhaust, the seasons have gradually shifted and some birds no longer know where to go to make their nests.

For example, in France, swallows have been sighted spending the winter in Normandy instead of Africa. It is predicted that by 2050 no swallows will migrate to warmer southern climates. With an average temperature increase of 4.5 degrees Fahrenheit throughout Europe, we'll even find exotic plants able to live in places that were usually too cold for them before.

So when spring comes around, birds may not be a sign of spring—though they will still be busy making nests to welcome their baby birds—unless antipollution measures like the ones adopted in Kyoto in 1997 and ratified by the European Union in 2002 succeed in halting these radical climate changes.

When did we skip directly from Thursday, October 4, to Friday, October 15?

For more than six thousand years, people have based the length of a year on the solar cycle, or, in other words, on the amount of time it takes the earth to rotate around the sun.

In ancient Egypt, a year lasted exactly 365 days, but the earth actually takes an extra quarter day to go around the sun.

This means that after four years the Egyptian calendar was off by one day (four times one quarter), after forty years by ten days, and after four hundred years by more than three months. At that rate, winter would soon wind up in August!

The Romans attempted to reestablish order: The Julian calendar introduced by Julius Caesar included 365.25 days, or 365 days for three years and 366 days every fourth year.

But they still hadn't gotten it quite right. The solar year actually lasts 365.242 days. To finally get an accurate calendar, Pope Gregory XIII declared 1582 a leap year, a year in which the month of February has twenty-nine days. There is a leap year every four years, three centuries out of four. And in order to make up for the lag accumulated under the Julian calendar, in 1582 the calendar skipped directly from Thursday, October 4, to Friday, October 15. Too bad for people born from the 5th to the 14th—that year they had to do without a birthday party!

When
do we have
fevers?

When everything is going well, our body temperature stays at about 98.6 degrees Fahrenheit. But if you have a cold, the flu, or a stomach virus, your temperature can suddenly shoot up. Fever is always a symptom of an infection or a virus.

Though it leaves us dizzy and sweaty and makes our teeth chatter, fever is very useful. It serves as our body's alarm signal to warn us that something is wrong.

Unless the fever climbs dangerously above 104 degrees Fahrenheit or it's too uncomfortable to handle, it's better not to use medicine to make it go down. Fever helps our body kill bacteria and viruses that poison our blood and assists the body in defending and healing itself.

Yet it's important to be careful if you have a fever. A particularly high fever can be dangerous due to the risk of convulsions (serious brain disturbances) or dehydration (lack of water in the body).

Here's some good advice: If you have a fever, don't forget to drink a lot, take baths, and avoid burying yourself in a pile of blankets so that your body won't overheat.

When will I stop being afraid of the dark?

Most of the time, so long as the sun is up and the lights are on, life is a walk in the park. But as soon as the lights are out and you have to go to sleep in the darkness of your room, dark and terrifying thoughts overpower you.

A floorboard creaks, you hear a strange little sound, and you panic! Though you may be cozy under the blankets, you feel as lost in your own room as you would in the most treacherous jungle.

When we can't see anything, we imagine the worst: monstrous creatures, burglars, witches. Our scariest demons close ranks and attack from all sides.

This unjustified fear of the dark is a leftover from our early childhood. Very young children constantly need their parents' affection and attention. When they start sleeping through the night, they dread the long period of separation they will have to get through alone until morning. They quickly start to associate night with the fear of being alone.

THERE'S SOMEONE BREATHING NEARBY.

I HEAR IT. WHO IS THAT? I'M SCARED.

Though we no longer dread the solitude of our bed as we grow older, we retain an apprehension of darkness that sometimes leads us to sleep with the curtains open and the nightlight on, even when we're all grown up.

When does the future start?

We live and act in an eternal present that we call "now" that transforms every passing hour, minute, and second into the past.

Whether something happened yesterday, the day before yesterday, three months ago, or five hours ago, we keep hold of these bygone moments as memories in our minds. These memories make up our histories. To remember is to bring the past back to life in our minds.

THE FUTURE DOESN'T EXIST.

JUST WAIT TILL NEXT WINTER.

NO FUTUR

But when does our future begin? That's a paradoxical question to which we might be tempted to answer "Never!" By definition, the future doesn't exist yet and never will exist. is always ahead of us, like the distant horizon on the trail of time we're following. It moves back with every step we take forward and never lets us catch up.

Yet even if our future and the future of humanity don't exist and can't be seen in a crystal ball, humans have always made their projections come true by dreaming of better tomorrows: making fire, flying, crossing the oceans, building cities, curing previously incurable illnesses, traveling into space.

The future is being built today, in our thoughts, dreams, and imagination.

When do tsunamis form?

Tsunami is a Japanese word that means "port wave." In English, we refer to it as a tidal wave. Tsunamis such as the terrible natural disaster that destroyed parts of Asia in December 2004 are actually underwater earthquakes.

Every day, every minute, some part of the earth is shaking. Sometimes it's a very slight remor that barely rattles the windows and goes unnoticed. Other times it's a real earthquake that devastates everything in its path.

Even if we don't realize it, the earth is always moving. Underground layers of rock shift and collide with varying degrees of violence.

The shock wave spreads over a circumference of several miles, provoking tremors of variable intensity. Seismologists (earthquake specialists) measure this intensity on a scale known as the Richter scale, which runs from one to nine. The higher the number, the stronger the earthquake.

When this shock wave takes place underwater, it creates giant waves that can travel at 500 to 560 miles per hour. They can be up to one hundred feet tall, or the equivalent of a ten-story building. When they reach the shore, they engulf and sweep away everything in their path.

STOP THROWING ROCKS! YOU COULD HURT SOMEONE!

When does a chameleon change colors?

There are about ninety different types of chameleons. Every one of them has the astonishing power to change colors in a few seconds.

This is why in Africa the chameleon is the messenger of the gods. The same colors as the rainbow, the chameleon is considered a link between the gods in the heavens and people on earth.

But how does such a small animal pull off such an amazing magic trick? In reality, the explanation has more to do with science than with magic or religion. Under its scaly, thick translucent skin, the chameleon has a whole range of cells full of coloring substances.

Through subtly complex chemical reactions, these multicolored cells can get bigger or smaller, extend or branch out, and cause light effects and reflections. The cells create a multitude of colorful combinations, like the endless variety of colors a painter creates when he mixes his pigments.

The chameleon can will itself to blend with the vegetation in order to hide from predators that want to eat it. But it can also become black with anger, white or spotted with yellow when it's scared, and brown when it's too hot. In other words, the chameleon "speaks" with the color of its skin.

When do they make
babies
in test tubes?

On July 25, 1978, a perfectly healthy girl named Louise Brown was born in England. For the first time in the history of humanity, an embryo had been conceived in a glass tube in a lab rather than in its mother's body.

This revolutionary technique, which is also known as "in vitro fertilization" and "medically assisted procreation," would allow many sterile couples (couples that cannot naturally reproduce) to have children.

The method consists of removing an ovum—the woman's reproductive cell—from the ovary and placing it inside a test tube with a spermatozoa from the husband or another man. Three days later, the fertilized egg is reimplanted in the mother's body.

This great medical "first" has led to the births of one and a half million "test tube babies" as healthy as naturally conceived children.

There is one peculiarity, however: The incidence of twins, triplets, and even greater combinations of siblings among test tube babies is particularly high. Since the implantation of the egg doesn't work every time, several eggs are placed in the mother at once. Sometimes these eggs lead to the birth of many babies!

AND HOW OLD DO I HAVE TO BE TO LEAVE THE TEST TUBE?

When it's noon in New York, what time is it in Tokyo?

The globe is divided into time zones separating the earth into twenty-four one-hour longitudinal "strips" that start at the Greenwich Meridian in a suburb of London.

Today, we take this efficient, simple time zone system for granted—yet it was only perfected in the late nineteenth century. Before then, when it came to telling the time, chaos reigned from one country to the next and even within a single country.

Each city used to set its clocks to the sun. There could be up to ten or fifteen minutes' difference from one town to the next. The railroads started using time zones to minimize travel confusion in 1883, and most of the United States followed. In 1918 Congress passed the Standard Time Act, which is the basis for the time zones we use today.

I MADE SURE TO CALL YOU AT EIGHT SO I WOULDN'T WAKE YOU.

YES, BUT I'M IN NEW YORK TODAY.

When you travel abroad or even across the country, you have to set your watch forward or backward to adjust to the time difference. If you travel to Los Angeles from New York, you set it back three hours. You set it forward six hours if you fly to Paris, or fourteen hours if you fly to Sydney, Australia.

And when it's noon in New York? It's exactly 1 A.M. the next day in Tokyo.

When does the brain start working?

From its position at the control board in our skull, the brain is the captain of our body.

It uses a network of nerves that connect it to all the parts of our body to guide and coordinate the activities of our organs, senses, and muscles. The brain is what allows us to feel, think, and move—in short, to live.

A future baby's brain is like a factory for producing neurons, the cells in our nervous system, at the astounding rate of 250,000 cells a minute until the seventeenth week of pregnancy. And even at that stage the brain isn't ready to work yet.

Though it does contain all the necessary cells to function, the cells still need to be connected by what we call synapses, a kind of microcable that links neurons together.

These synapses form throughout the last two trimesters of the pregnancy and after the baby is born, thanks to the wealth of sensory experiences provided by the baby's surroundings—the taste of milk, the smell of its parents, the sounds of the house, the pleasant feeling of being caressed and held. All these discoveries stimulate the development of the newborn's brain, which will continue throughout the childhood years and even after.

When do wasps sting?

Even though wasps look very elegant with their narrow waists and black and yellow stripes, nobody likes it when they invite themselves to our picnics and summer barbecues. If they aren't satisfied with raiding our cold cuts and desserts, they come after us!

LET'S STOP.

THERE'S NO MORE ROOM.

But why do they attack our skin? They don't do it to feed on our blood, like mosquitoes do, but to defend themselves if they've been disturbed while collecting food.

Our friend the wasp doesn't have any time to waste: It has to bring food back to the hive to feed the larvae laid by the queen.

To prevent getting stung, avoid attracting wasps by covering sweet foods like jam and fresh fruit and don't make any sudden gestures if they are around. In most cases, they'll buzz off after a few minutes to find food elsewhere.

No matter what happens, don't panic. A wasp sting is not serious, unless you're stung in the mouth or you're severely allergic. But be careful anyhow—a wasp has more than one trick up its stinger and can strike its victim several times in a row.

When was God born?

According to theologians (philosophers and specialists of religion) and believers all over the world, God was never born and will never die because an infinite being doesn't have a beginning or an end.

God escapes fate and somehow exists outside of the flow of life in an unchanging, unalterable eternity.

Though the existence of God is based on the absence of a beginning and an end, it is possible to consider the beginning of the *idea* of God as people have conceived it over the centuries.

The first religions were polytheistic ones that believed in several gods. The first monotheistic religions, which hold that there is only one God, were Judaism and Christianity, which were followed by Islam in the Middle Ages. These religions quickly took on a growing importance in people's lives, dictating the way they should behave and organizing the calendar based on religious feasts and rituals. Even kings proclaimed they were chosen by God.

In the West, politics have gradually separated from religion in the last century or two and believing in God is no longer a matter of state, but a private one.

When I have to speak in front of people, why am I scared?

Sharing secrets with your friends, telling your parents what you did all day, joking with your sister, or hiding behind your math book to gossip in the back of the classroom—sometimes it seems a lot harder to keep quiet than to talk. Talking is part of what defines us as humans. Exchanging information with those we're close to is second nature.

But things get a little more complicated when it comes to uncomfortable situations like speaking in public, standi in front of your whole class, having to make conversatio with a humorless old uncle at the dinner table.

It's as if your voice, which is generally so fluid, suddenly gets stuck at the back of your throat. You stutter, blush, lose your cool, and can't find your words. You are paralyzed at the thought that you look out of place or ridiculous. In fact, you're just scared.

Scared? Of what? Scared of not expressing yourself properly, looking foolish in front of others, saying something stupid, accidentally revealing your most secret feelings—in other words, you're scared of getting caught being yourself.

SO ARE YOU GOING TO SING OR WHAT?

I'M NERVOUS!

We dread speaking in any circumstance when our words commit us to something; when we know that people will use what we say to assess, judge, admire, or criticize us. Immediately! On your words!

When did we understand that zero isn't nothing?

YOU INVENTED THE ZERO, SO YOU'RE GOING TO EXPLAIN THIS TO MY DAD.

For thousands of years, zero didn't exist. People didn't see the use of inventing a number that represented nothing.

Zero first appeared in the second century BCE in Babylon but wasn't considered a number yet. It only served to designate the absence of a unit in a given rank: In 101, the zero represented the absence of a unit of ten.

Three minus three equals zero. Seems obvious, right? Yet it was by doing this problem that Brahmagupta, an Indian mathematician in the sixth century CE, turned zero into a full-fledged number. The number zero appeared in the Arab world in the eighth century, after being introduced to the court of Caliph Al-Mansur of Baghdad by an Indian astronomer. It only began spreading through Europe in the twelfth century, and even then people were reluctant to use the number because they saw it as a symbol of nothing, a disturbing void sent directly from the devil.

Yet zero was far from nonexistent or harmful. Its introduction in calculations led to tremendous progress in algebra, which was in turn the basis for fundamental advances in the fields of science, astrology, architecture, economy, and mechanics, right down to computers, which run on a binary language, a coded sequence of ones and zeros.

When someone **attacks me,** how should I defend myself?

STOP OR I'LL TELL MY DAD!

I'M SOOO SCARED!

KARATE CLUB

Whether you're throwing punches, kicks, or judo or karate moves, sometimes fighting is just for fun. Disagreements between friends often come to a friendly resolution with a mutual decision to make peace.

When you get attacked, when those preying on you are more numerous or stronger than you and are determined to put you through the wringer, it's no joke.

Schoolyard extortion, bullying, theft, intimidation, harassment, insults, teasing. How do you defend yourself against this kind of violence when you happen to feel defenseless?

If you respond to violence with violence, you can be sure things will only get worse. But if you give in because you think you don't have a chance, you become an easy target and your tormentors have an open invitation to keep picking on you.

The only solution in these cases is to speak to an adult who will know what to do to put a stop to this intolerable situation. Telling a grown-up that someone stronger, older, or more popular is picking on you isn't being a tattletale. By doing so, you shatter the terrible law of silence that allows bullies to prey on other kids without fear of the consequences.

When did we start flushing the toilet?

Not so long ago, toilets were nothing more than holes in the ground—outside, fortunately! After centuries of using open chairs with chamber pots underneath and outhouses in the backyard, people were delighted with the enormous progress that brought them locking bathrooms with toilet paper and flush toilets.

The first flush toilet was perfected in 1595 by an English lord, John Harington, to please his godmother, Queen Elizabeth I of England.

GREAT, NOW WE JUST NEED TO FLUSH HIM OUT.

PLOP

Yet his invention did not meet with any success outside of the royal palace because houses at that time weren't yet equipped with the vast network of sewage pipes we use to evacuate dirty water.

It wasn't until sewage pipes were installed in urban centers in the late nineteenth century that Harington's invention became common in houses and apartment buildings, gradually replacing chamber pots and outdoor bathroom ditches in cities and, eventually, the countryside.

Yet in some countries water remains too rare and precious to use to evacuate bodily waste. Homes in these countries do not include the flush toilet as one of their standard amenities.

When did people start living together?

Everyone has dreamed of living alone on a deserted island like Robinson Crusoe at one time or another.

Yet aside from hermits and characters in novels, few people really enjoy being alone for more than a few hours at a time.

STARTING TODAY YOU'RE GOING TO CALL ME KING AND WE'RE GOING TO LIVE IN A SOCIETY!

Since the beginning of history, humans have grouped together to share the warmth of a fire and the food they scavenged and hunted, and to protect themselves from wild animals. In the Neolithic Age, our distant ancestors settled in permanent villages and formed small hierarchical societies.

Over the centuries, human societies kept growing and refining their organization. Roles gradually became specialized, with each member of the society taking the place granted to him or her by rank, skill, and gender. This differentiation made it possible to diversify human activities, but it also created inequalities between the rich and the poor and those who led and those who merely followed.

Starting in the eighteenth century, the idea that all people should live free and equal in society began taking hold both in America and Europe. Democracies replaced divine right monarchies. Though there are still inequalities and injustices, democracy remains a great way of organizing life in a society. But it is a fragile system that must be defended to maintain the ideals of freedom and equality on which it is founded.

When do people get old?

We start aging—and therefore getting old—from the day we're born!

But we're only genuinely old once we're senior citizens and we've lived through childhood and the "prime of life," our adult years. Our cells gradually stop reproducing, our muscles become smaller, and our skin visibly wrinkles.

In "developed" nations, people live longer thanks to medical advances and more comfortable living conditions. People want to "stay young," or at least look young, as long as possible.

PEOPLE ARE OLD WHEN THEY HAVE PIMPLES LIKE MY SISTER!

Though old age is natural, we've gradually come to see it as a kind of decline. We believe we should struggle to erase the passage of time and the differ-ences between generations. Yet we often forget that genuine youth is more closely related to the mind—which can remain curious and open to the world regardless of how much time passes—than to the body, which ages no matter what we do.

In Africa, on the other hand, old age is seen as a source of wisdom. The "councils of wise men" that rule over village life consist of the oldest men in the community. In Japan, younger generations have enormous respect for their elders and turn to them for comfort and good advice.

When **does** lightning strike?

WE HAVE TO WAIT FOR LIGHTNING TO STRIKE.

SO ARE YOU GETTING THE FIRE GOING OR WHAT?

When there's a storm, you can measure how far away it is by counting the number of seconds between the flash of lightning that streaks across the sky and the sound of rumbling thunder.

Sound travels about one thousand feet in one second while lightning is visible practically instantly: Multiply one thousand by the number of seconds you counted and you can determine how many feet separate you from the place where lightning struck.

Lightning used to terrify prehistoric people because they didn't know how to protect themselves from it. But by setting trees ablaze it gave them fire long before they had discovered how to produce it by rubbing flints together. The people of ancient times used to believe that lightning was a sign of the gods' anger sent to earth to punish them or warn them to behave themselves.

Humans later learned to protect themselves from these electric bolts from the sky by installing lightning rods on their rooftops.

Though lightning is a dangerous natural force that sets trees on fire and electrocutes people with massive electric shocks, there's one thunderbolt that remains entirely pleasant: the thunderbolt that hits us when we fall in love at first sight!

When do we stop needing our parents?

Even though baby birds eagerly wait to be fed and small mammals can't survive without maternal milk, after a few hours, days, or months every animal manages to spread its wings and fly without its parents' help. Every animal except the human.

Before it can face the world and its dangers alone and provide for itself, a young human must go through long years of apprenticeship: about a year to stand on its own two feet, two to start talking, three to keep itself clean, five or six to go to school, and eighteen to be an adult in the eyes of the law.

According to scientists, the young human takes a longer time to acquire complete autonomy than other animals because it is more intelligent. Its brain, which is more developed and complex, needs longer to reach its maximum potential.

MAYBE IT'S TIME TO TELL HIM TO LEAVE HOME?

In so-called developed societies, comfortable living conditions allow young people to keep studying into their twenties. These years of schooling are constantly growing longer, making children financially dependent on their parents for a longer time. In more traditional societies, the adolescent stage doesn't exist. People pass from childhood to adulthood around thirteen or fourteen through initiation ceremonies that represent the passage into the "grown-up" world.

Yet once we're adults, we always think about our parents, even after their deaths, because they've left us the legacy of their histories, their values, and their love.

When
will my parents
trust me?

"Don't come home too late!" "Do your homework!" Sometimes you feel like responding to your parents' constant orders and nervous questions by hanging a sign around your neck: "Trust me and give me some space!"

When will your parents finally understand that you can manage your school-work and stay home alone without flooding the bath-room or burning your breakfast?

But the reason par-ents are overly protective of their children isn't that they don't trust them. It's because they love them so much. The parent-child rela-tionship is a long story of gradual sepa-ration. As in every love story, it's hard to be separated from those you love.

Parents mostly tend to be on their kids' backs because of worry. They're always worried some-thing bad is going to happen to them.

To get your parents to have blind faith in you—or at least something approaching it— you need to show them that you're mature enough to take care of yourself without putting yourself in harm's way. If you haven't done so already, it's up to you to gain your parents' trust.

Index by Subject